MARRIED TO BORDERLINE PERSONALITY DISORDER

Your BPD Stories of Roses and Rage

ROBERT PAGE

Book #3 in the *Roses and Rage BPD* Series

For more information about Robert Page:
amazon.com/author/robertpagewriter
or email: robertpagewriter@gmail.com
And join the Facebook support group: Roses and Rage: Spouses of Borderline Personality Disorder

Print version ISBN-13 9798682897018

CONTENTS

INTRODUCTION

"You are not alone." When I wrote those words in the previous two entries of the *Roses and Rage BPD* series, they felt too simplistic. Desiring to consistently write with some gravitas, I crafted several replacement sentences, but they all ended up requiring far more words to describe the same result.

I ultimately retreated to my first instincts, and your reaction to the earlier books has proven the point: most spouses of a BP (someone with Borderline Personality Disorder) indeed feel *desperately* alone.

Each week, I am contacted by readers using self-descriptive terms like "crushed," "humiliated," "baffled," and "beaten." But always the great unifier is "alone."

More often than not, readers like you (the non-BPs) describe for me a pattern of growing awareness. Early in the relationship, you are convinced that *you* are the cause of the current hellscape. Only through a helpful reference to BPD made by a friend, colleague, or therapist did an alternate narrative present itself.

The next step for many of you is a quick internet search and a few blog articles, after which the symptoms of BPD begin to stand out as eerily familiar. You need more information, but still want to stay mostly under the radar so as to not trigger your spouse's alarms.

A search for books turns up several choices that seem to offer explanations and possibly even solutions. Perhaps you were drawn to the titles in my series because, unlike most of what is available, they are written specifically for BP spouses in a non-clinical, compassionate style.

The point of *Could Your Spouse Have Borderline Personality Disorder?* is to provide a down-and-dirty street guide to BPD without any fluff. I saw a need for a bridge between brief website articles and overly complex books written by scholars trying to impress other scholars.

I also wanted to provide an introductory guide that was inexpensive and therefore more accessible to readers on a budget. Wonderfully, I received several reviews and emails stating, "Love the content, but IT'S TOO SHORT!" This naturally led me to the second book in the series.

BPD from the Husband's POV is the full-combo meal when it comes to information for a BP spouse. I amplified all the non-clinical content from *Could Your Wife* and added many more true-life examples as well as the invaluable "What I Wish I Had Done" inserts.

Reader response to book #2 has been overwhelmingly positive. BP spouses finally had a book written just for them by one of their own. And even though my target audience was spouses of BPs, I am exceedingly pleased to find that BPs have been drawn to the book as well. I'm happy to help people on both sides of the same coin.

With the passage of time, I've noticed patterns in how readers respond to the information they acquire from my books and other sources. Like most spouses new to BPD, you start playing the game where you see how many of the symptoms match up to your spouse's behavior. Your eyebrows raise a little higher with each check mark.

Amazed that you might not be the sole cause of the gasoline constantly being flung on your heated relationship, some of you make the crucial error of rushing to your spouse with a book in hand declaring, "Good news honey, I figured out that the reason for all our problems is *your* personality disorder!" Whoops. Too much, too soon.

Unlike some of my overly excited readers (and I'm guilty as well), I hope you avoid that "special" moment of BP retaliation.

It's probably best to remain in stealth mode while you gather more information and seek help from others who have more experience.

Within the realization that the problems in your relationship have a name (BPD) and that thousands of other spouses out there are going through your exact checklist of symptoms is a beautiful message of hope. Why? Because (you guessed it), you are not alone.

You are now a member of a special tribe—the spouses of BPD. It's not a group to which you ever hoped to be awarded membership, in fact, none of us would have chosen to be here, just as BPs wouldn't choose to have a personality disorder, but we might as well help each other as best we can. Welcome my friend; we saved you a chair.

Which leads us to the purpose of this book—learning from others just like you but who have been sitting in the clubhouse a bit longer.

◆ ◆ ◆

Why This Book?

I originally had no idea if readers would respond, but in the early printings of my first two BPD books, I provided an email address and said, "Reach out to tell me your story and maybe I'll use it in a book." It was a true surprise when the emails started coming in, and they've never stopped.

When reading your letters, I was quickly reminded what so many BP spouses/significant-others go through that unifies all of us. Confusion, shame, anger, accusations, financial loss, family trauma, criminal charges, child custody battles, feeling helpless while witnessing our life-partner being ripped apart from the inside— these are a sampling of BPD traits that bind us together.

"Getting if off my chest" was a common motivation for many of you, and I greatly appreciate you taking the time to share your BPD experiences with me, and now a selection of those experiences will be passed on to others within these pages.

The opinions and accounts in my previous writings were basically all my own, and the catharsis I felt was profound. Wonderfully, readers like you also benefited from knowing they weren't alone in their BPD existence. But now, it's time to expand on my initial impulse.

In this book, we hear primarily from YOU, the spouses of BPD who know what life in the trenches of personality disorder is truly like. You vividly understand the specific kind of biting honesty that can only come from others in your special tribe.

Clinicians strive to help others, but often can't avoid communicating in a style that is best suited for their peers at the next academic conference. Meanwhile, BPD memoirs make for interesting reading, but that's not the viewpoint that, as a BPD spouse, you strongly relate to. I don't want to write about those perspectives, and frankly, I don't think you want to read about them, or you wouldn't be here with me now.

Be aware, this is not a mindfulness workbook or behavioral cure-all. This book is all about intense, true-life accounts from others in your situation that can lead to an improved understanding of, and response to, borderline personality disorder.

♦ ♦ ♦

The Book Layout

The featured voice throughout these pages is not going to be mine. Unlike my other BPD books, I am turning the microphone over to my readers who have shared their words with me about living among those with a personality disorder.

I will serve more as a moderator who tries to connect the narrative with personal insight or relevant outside expertise. Also, there are many excellent resources available that I occasionally turn to for "big picture" perspective. And yes, I'll throw in some of my personal anecdotes when it directly relates (such as the beginning of the next chapter that offers a *very* brief summary of BPD symptoms).

Many BPD-related books tend to be organized around the most common symptoms of the disorder. Each chapter presents a symptom, gives examples of behavior, and discusses coping methods. The pattern repeats, and soon enough there is a complete book.

Since this book is driven more by the random narrative supplied to me by readers, it's not always possible to deliver the content in easily categorized chunks. In this case, the river simply flows to the path of least resistance, which is not always where I might have expected. I consider it appropriate for me to not fight that current. Rather, I'm taking the role of a kayaker who can adjust for temporary speed and approach, but the general direction and destination are out of my control.

This take-it-as-it-comes approach is much in line with the subject we are dealing with—borderline personality disorder and all of the unpredictable disruption it causes.

If you would also like a more conventional path that breaks down the accepted descriptions of BPD symptoms, take a look in my other books, or consult the back of this book for suggested readings.

But for those of us ready to learn from what other spouses of borderline personality disorder have experienced firsthand, let's get started.

A Brief Note for Those with Borderline Personality

I want to welcome those with BPD who read books like this hoping to gain insight as to what their significant others are thinking.

Those are good instincts, and I applaud you for seeking answers. However, there will almost certainly be content ahead that will be triggering and upsetting to those with BPD. I'd like you to know that I have nothing but respect for you and your feelings, but BP spouses deserve a place to share their own truth without restraint, and I'm here to facilitate that, so keep your mind open and let's try to give the spouses a safe space.

CHAPTER 1: WHAT IS BPD (AND KEEP IT SHORT)?

"If you leave, I will kill myself RIGHT THIS MINUTE!"

At the time my wife screamed those words at me, I really didn't understand what I was dealing with. Like most spouses of someone with borderline personality disorder, I didn't know I was one. I had to learn the truth through a painful series of baby steps, giant steps, and many missteps.

Maybe you've already done some internet research and have begun thinking your spouse has BPD. The problem is, most Borderlines refuse to be diagnosed, so you are left to find information on your own, usually in secret because your spouse would not approve.

Before we hear from the many readers who have contributed to this book, we need to acquire some basic understanding of BPD. Some of you may be reading about these concepts for the first time and need the overview. For others, don't worry, I'll keep it short.

What Is Borderline Personality Disorder?
BPD belongs to a broader category called "Personality Disorders." Other members of this group include bi-polar personality disorder and narcissistic personality disorder (there are others as well).

The "bible" used in the psychiatric profession to identify personality disorders is the *Diagnostic and Statistical Manual* known simply as the *DSM*. It receives occasional updates, and the editions I draw from are the fourth and fifth.

The *DSM-IV* lists nine symptoms of BPD in dry but mostly comprehensible language. It states that clinicians should determine at least five of the nine symptoms are present before a positive diagnosis can be made. That's surprisingly simple for the layperson to understand — so of course the powers-that-be had to muck it up.

The DSM-5 (I have no idea why they switched from Roman numerals to Arabic), attempts to amplify and "improve" the list of symptoms, with mixed results. It gives clinicians more freedom to diagnose without the "5 of 9" mandate, but it also makes it harder for people on the street to use.

With that bit of background out of the way, the *DSM-IV* tells us that BPD is:

A pervasive pattern of instability of interpersonal relationships, self-image, and affects, and marked impulsivity beginning by early adulthood and present in a variety of contexts.

Like I mentioned; the language is clinical. Let's run it through a real-world filter.

What is the Non-clinical Definition of BPD?

I would focus on the keywords "pervasive" and "variety." If the various symptoms listed between those two words aren't happening regularly and in lots of different places, we're not talking about BPD.

You may be experiencing some messed up behavior, but it falls under some other category or it's just someone who is basically a jerk.

Makes sense, right? All of us might experience *some* BPD-like symptoms *some* of the time. But with a BP the traits are intense and present *much* of the time. Keep in mind that a BP isn't likely to have *all* of the symptoms *all* the time, so don't get confused if your spouse doesn't get a check mark in each column (that's actually a good thing).

So, what are these traits and symptoms? Let's break them down.

Symptom #1: Fear of Abandonment

Fear of abandonment results in unstable, intense, and conflicted close relationships, marked by mistrust, neediness, and anxious preoccupation with real or imagined abandonment (*DSM-5*).

The scariest part for the BP spouse with regards to the above description is "real or imagined." If the BP is in a full-on abandonment rage, you are basically screwed no matter what you do.

If you actually committed an act to trigger the event — screwed.

If you actually committed no act whatsoever — yup, still screwed.

In my marriage to Lyssa (not her real name), her fear of abandonment escalated over the years to include things like:

· blocking doorways to keep me trapped in a room
· taking my car keys
· extensive verbal abuse in the form of insults and beratement
· threating several times to commit suicide

· jumping on the hood of my moving car to keep me from leaving

In *Stop Walking on Eggshells: Taking Your Life Back When Someone You Care About Has Borderline Personality Disorder*, authors Paul Mason and Randi Kreger quote a BP who says:

"When I feel abandoned, I feel a combination of isolation, terror, and alienation. I panic. I feel betrayed and used. I think I'm going to die."

I believe fear of abandonment is the foremost symptom a BP may present. I put that last sentence in bold so you won't miss how important it is. If the BP in your life begins spinning out of control, more often than not you are witnessing an extreme expression of "don't leave me" even if their behavior is forcing you to do just that.

If you want more examples of this and all the other symptoms, don't worry, that's what the rest of the book is about. For now, let's keep reviewing the basic descriptions of BPD traits.

Symptom #2: Extreme Viewpoint

The BP will often view close relationships in extremes of idealization and devaluation and alternating between over involvement and withdrawal (*DSM-5*).

The act of a BP swinging wildly between idolizing and demonizing a person is called *splitting*. The BP will likely base their feelings about you on the most current interaction the two of you have had. Past actions don't count for much so don't expect credit for time served.

A BP who is splitting sees only good or evil and has no memory of previously assigning one label to a person while in the clutch of the polar opposite. The BP exists in an all-or-nothing world.

When a BP thinks you have committed even a slight infraction, the only choice for them is to fully demonize you. In one moment, you're a hero and a perfect life-partner. Then in the next, they are disgusted at the thought of being married to someone so unworthy.

It can take hours or days, but eventually your spouse sees actions from you that earn your promotion back to "angel" status. In the meantime, your head is spinning as you try to keep up.

Symptom #3: Mood Swings
A BP will experience frequent mood changes; emotions that are easily aroused, intense, and/or out of proportion to events and circumstances (*DSM-5*).

You may be noticing that some BPD symptoms overlap. This is certainly true of a BP's tendency to view the world in extremes and have mood swings.

A BP will move swiftly from calm to calamity. To the spouse, the rapid swings are exhausting.

There were several nights Lyssa subjected me to sleep deprivation by ripping the bedding and sheets away from me, turning on all the lights in the house, yanking pillows from under my head, and insisting that I engage her in an argument.

The outcome? I would eventually become angry and stay that way for days, while her mood would quickly swing back to pleasant. The next day, she would criticize me for still being upset and insist I owed her an apology. Sound familiar to your life?

Symptom #4: Unstable Relationships

The BP often experiences fears of rejection by — and/or separation from — significant others, associated with fears of excessive dependency and complete loss of autonomy (*DSM-5*).

People with BPD are prone to enter quickly into romantic relationships. They become convinced that this devotee will deliver all the love they seek.

Merri Lisa Johnson, in *Girl in Need of a Tourniquet: Memoir of a Borderline Personality*, describes her need for love this way:

"I need to hear the words. 'You win the prize. I will love you forever. You are worth losing everything else.' Jackpot. Home base. An umpire whispers in my ear, 'You're safe.'"

Yet, in a twist of self-destruction, the BP will often crash and burn a relationship only to try and start it again. If their partner obliges, the cycle will continue with great dramatic affect.

In a marriage, ceasing the relationship is arduous to say the least. Instead, the BP tends to create considerable havoc within a household because the tensions are not released through absence. Perhaps you've heard the expression, "fighting like two cats in a bag?"

Symptom #5: Distorted Self-Image

The BP will often present a markedly impoverished, poorly developed, or unstable self-image (*DSM-5*). In other words, the BP's self-image stops forming before it is able to fully take hold.

I know this is difficult for a non-BP to grasp, but try to consider how terrifying it must feel to not be sure that you exist except for how others see you. Take away "others" and what happens to a BP? Poof! They see themselves as obliterated. Do you notice how this connects back to a fear of abandonment? If you leave, they disappear.

Your spouse compensates by finding identity through *you*. They repeatedly declare, "I'd be lost without you." That's no lie.

Because the BP is adept at co-opting the best elements of someone else's self-image, the BP is often viewed by others as likeable and fun. After all, who wouldn't want to be around a positive version of themselves?

The challenge for the non-BP spouse becomes trying to convince others of what you face in your private marriage. They see your spouse as healthy and happy, and your stories of despair and rage don't seem authentic. To the casual observer, it's *you* who appears to be the troubled one, not your spouse.

Many of you just mentally shouted, "HE'S TALKING ABOUT ME!" I have been there dear friend, and I understand.

Many BP spouses learn to keep their anguish to themselves and become all the more isolated. By this point, the personality disorder begins to dominate the marriage. The bizarre becomes normal.

Symptom #6: Impulsive Behaviors

BPs often act on the spur of the moment in response to immediate stimuli; acting on a momentary basis without a plan or consideration of outcomes (*DSM-5*).

How would you react if you found your husband had smashed yet another car or drained the savings account on a gambling spree? What if your wife maxed out a credit card you didn't even know about? Or what if she's pregnant by another man and declares it's your fault for not being a better lover?

For the BP caught up in this symptom, there is no before or after, only now, and the now is often distressing. With less ability to incorporate the before and after (i.e., consequences) into current actions, a BP is more likely to say, "I want more!"

To make matters worse, after the BP comes down from the high of their impulsive behaviors, they tend to underrate the gravity of what happened. While you're left to mop up a calamitous mess, your spouse is saying, "I don't know what the big deal is."

Symptom #7: Self-harm

BPs will often engage in dangerous, risky, and potentially self-damaging activities, unnecessarily and without regard to consequences; lack of concern for one's limitations and denial of the reality of personal danger (*DSM-5*).

At first glance, this looks similar to the symptom of impulsiveness we just discussed. The difference is that those were actions that *might* cause physical harm. Now we're talking about actions *designed* to cause harm.

The types of self-harm associated with BP behavior may include:
--cutting
--skin scratching
--head banging (not the heavy metal kind)
--hair pulling

--tearing off scabs
--needle poking
--burning
--biting
--breaking bones

In *Girl in Need of a Tourniquet*, Merri Lisa Johnson describes her self-harm as a message of self-loathing:

"I want to tell them I carve scarlet letters in my skin like hate mail in the dead letter office of my body."

BPs are drawn to living in the now, but without a strong sense of self, even the now can feel miserable. Self-harm gives the now meaning. For a fleeting instant, there is a sensation of feeling blissfully alive.

Symptom #8: Suicide

The BP may have frequent feelings of being down, miserable, and/or hopeless; difficulty recovering from such moods; pessimism about the future; pervasive shame; feeling of inferior self-worth; thoughts of suicide and suicidal behavior (*DSM-5*).

Of all the BPD traits I faced with my wife Lyssa, her multiple suicidal threats were the scariest. I had no training or experience with what I was confronted by and failed miserably at being helpful.

An often-quoted statistic is that 8–10 percent of people with borderline personality disorder commit suicide. That's not attempting suicide, but actually succeeding.

From the very first instance of suicidal behavior in my marriage, I should have reached out for help. Or at the very least, I should have expressed to Lyssa in a calm moment that any future mention of suicide would result in an emergency 911 call. No exceptions.

According to the National Institute of Mental Health, the spouse of a BP should:

"Take seriously any comments about suicide or wishing to die. Even if you do not believe your family member or friend will attempt suicide, the person is clearly in distress and can benefit from your help in finding treatment."

Help can be found by calling the National Suicide Prevention Lifeline toll-free at 1–800–273–TALK (8255), 24 hours a day, 7 days a week. The deaf and hard of hearing can contact the lifeline via TTY at 1–800–799–4889. All calls are free and confidential. If you are still in contact with the BP in your life, load these numbers into your cell phone just in case.

Symptom #9: Anger
The BP may demonstrate persistent or frequent angry feelings; anger or irritability in response to minor slights and insults (*DSM-5*).

If you're married to a BP, you are quite familiar with the concept of unpredictable and inconsolable rage. It is an awesome spectacle to behold and terrible to be on the receiving end of.

For the BP, there is no "ramping up," but instead an immediate leap from a state of relative calm to that of blind rage. And as a spouse, the focus of this emotional storm is usually straight at you.

Here is a sample list of events that sparked off-the-hook anger in my marriage:

--I laughed at a mildly sexual joke on the *Simpsons* TV show
--I asked a stranger (of the opposite sex) for directions
--I high-fived someone (of the opposite sex)
--I didn't look away from Victoria's Secret commercial on TV
--I looked away from a Victoria's Secret commercial on TV in a way that made fun of the fact that she insisted I look away (Petty, I know, but it happens even in the best of marriages).

Throughout these events, there were personal letters destroyed, computer documents altered, friends "unfriended," emails sent falsely representing me, and one time she even kicked in an entire kitchen wall.

During the "morning after" of her rage-attacks, she would hardly acknowledge anything had happened. If I challenged her detachment she would glibly say, "You need to learn how to let go."

Symptom #10: Dissociation
The BP may demonstrate transient, stress-related paranoid ideation or severe dissociative symptoms (*DSM-IV*).

In simpler terms, when the BP experiences symptoms too intense for their psyche to handle, they simply shut down. Like an engine protecting itself from overheating, the system shifts into "safety mode" until the threat diminishes.

Talking to a BP in this state is incredibly confusing for a spouse. Attempts to address recent conflicts or bad behavior are met with blank stares or even complete denial.

To you and me, it appears that the BP is flagrantly lying. We ask ourselves, "How could they not remember the awful things that were said and done?"

Dissociation is not a ruse meant to consciously dodge responsibility (although a BP will do that too). It's quite likely they just can't focus on the details clearly enough to feel confident about the facts.

Remember, a BP usually walks and talks like a completely normal person. But on the inside, they are not well. The word disorder is in the name of their ailment for a reason. Sometimes their brains just cannot engage the connections that would make life easier.

An Important Note on Compassion

After reviewing the list of BPD symptoms and some of their consequences, you might start to feel considerable antagonism towards your spouse. You may feel a great need to assign blame. That is *not* what this book is about. If you're simply looking for justification to shout at your spouse, "It's all your fault and you don't deserve my love," then put this down right now and go on your way because I don't want to be involved.

Your spouse does not choose to have BPD. They do not choose to feel terrified when they think you might abandon them. They did not marry you hoping to create a quagmire of relationship dread. She or he married you because of a beautiful thing we call love and the desire to share all things big and small with a special someone.

For the BP, there is rarely, if ever, a preconceived deception at work. The eventual results may be catastrophic, but the original intentions were purely innocent.

With this in mind, empathy and compassion should be the highest priority of a BP spouse until self preservation or physical safety is in peril.

You should always strive to stay calm in the face of BP traits. You will often fail, I certainly did. But that doesn't mean you shouldn't keep trying to remember that the reason the two of you came together was glorious, profound, and immeasurable love.

CHAPTER 2: EARLY ON

A Note on the Content from Readers

Many of the letters I receive from readers are casual in nature, often containing emoticons, mis-spellings, lack of capitalization, and incorrect or missing punctuation. This is typical of current communication styles found in social-media posts, internet messaging, and texting but doesn't always read well when copied into a book.

In other words, some edits by me were required. I cleaned up various problems that might lead to confusion but left intact many technically incorrect spellings and grammar choices. So, even though these excerpts might grate on the English teachers out there, I feel this is the best way to maintain the contributor's "voice" and spirit of the moment.

For the record, uncited quotes are drawn from emails sent to me from readers, online reviews from my books, direct messages sent through social media, and comments from my Facebook group "Roses and Rage: Spouses of Borderline Personality Disorder." The names of all these contributors as well as any self-identifying descriptions have been changed. All other quotes are cited where they appear.

This chapter features content referring to the pre-marriage stages of a relationship with a BP. Perhaps you will be reminded of what you went through in those challenging days.

Let's start with a letter from Barry who reached out for insight about what he might expect from his BPD relationship in the months ahead.

2 years ago, I met the most wonderful woman and she let me know of her BPD. I was so in love with her I was willing to go through anything to be with her.

She has left 2 times. Once for 3 months and come back and we worked on things and it seemed to get better and then it happened again and she left again for almost a month.

She returned and we felt more in love and even got engaged. All seemed perfect, but suddenly it crumbled and she started to get counseling and pushed me away and said she only had time for her and our little one.

I felt rejected and disregarded. Then she needed me and I asked her if she wanted me to stay with her and she pushed me away, so I left and went to a friend and left her and she harmed herself.

I feel like crap. Now she tells me, "Thank you. Your actions showed me what I truly mean to you," and she is leaving again.

Is loving someone with this disorder always this painful? Do you think it is the end of the line for my efforts? Thanks for reading and any advice because I am just drained.

It seems that Barry's love interest is presenting several BP traits including fear of abandonment, unstable relationships, and mood swings. This is especially represented by her wanting to hear how much he needs her, only to leave him soon after.

Another reader, Connor, saw Barry's post and gave his thoughts about if there will always be so much pain:

The short answer is yes. You will probably always have this level of pain in a relationship with someone with BPD.

The other thought I would share as someone who has been married to someone with this disorder for 26 years is you can't fix them. Unless she is willing to recognize that she has this problem and gets intense counseling and commits to working on it, for your own emotional and mental well-being I would not continue.

Even if she does get help, to me it is not clear she can ever be well and have a healthy relationship with you or anyone. It is terrible for them, more so than for you, but now that you are aware, you do have a choice. She does not.

Connor hits on an important point—the real victim of BPD is the person who has it. The non-BP ultimately has a choice to maintain contact with the source of the problem, or not. The BP, however, cannot simply sever the difficulties and "turn them off." The volume can be turned down and managed, but it does not disappear.

Have you ever found yourself in situation where your BP spouse refuses to let you sleep? Peter told me his version of a story I know quite well:

She wouldn't let me sleep because I would not admit fault and/or apologize for some imagined transgression. I would walk around exhausted for weeks at a time. She insisted I attend an anger management support group (twice!) because of "my" anger issue.

The full story is written elsewhere, but I actually *did* have to attend 10 weeks of anger management classes in order to have bogus charges of Felony Domestic Violence purged from my record. Week after week I sat around a table with a bunch of other men who all felt like losers as we were asked to draw pictures of birds or trees and talk about how they made us feel. At that moment, the horrific waste of my time was the only thing I was angry about.

Moving on, Stanley is the only reader who shared with me a series of texts in real-time as he was receiving them from his BP girlfriend. The intensity is palpable and her messages are rife with uncertainty as she refers to restraining orders and exhaustion.

[First text arrives]

You are temporarily unblocked. I replied to latest email. Contact before I file tonight.

[8 minutes later]

I barely had 3 hours of sleep last night...you've put me thru the ringer. Now, call me back, else I will submit the docs for 3 attorneys, based on your unfortunate decisions. Restraining order starts first. Then you counter sue. You said you have a three-day weekend.

[1 minute later]

I'm not messing with this anymore. Reach me sober and alone tonight, else I will see you in court.

[1 minute later]

It's only 5:30. This should be easy for you?

[5 minutes later]

I will relocate your cell and file at 7. I've been surviving with nothing, am exhausted. I refuse to delay into weekend. Make your choice and signal me. Else I will upload the docs and off we go.

[17 minutes later]

I will file tonight.

[4 minutes later and displaying uncertainty]

Wait...of course, 3-day weekend, you are probably with the drunk...Great! I will send my own licensed law enforcement to oversee access to my things.

[And finally, 6 minutes later and a complete reversal]

Just realized where you are. Never mind.

We can vividly visualize the torment she experiences as she continues to text Stanley and he remains silent. As her fear of abandonment builds, she gets more aggressive and ready to punish him for ignoring her. But in the end, she ponders if she might be pushing him too far and backs off...and the cycle likely will begin again for Stanley and his partner.

The next reader we will hear from is Connie who posted an all-too-common description of BPD emotional contradiction.

My girlfriend has been diagnosed BPD. Mostly she is the sweetest most loving woman, very articulate and very intelligent.

THEN some tiny insignificant thing may happen and suddenly she is a demon and goes on rants about other things such as the house is a mess, I'm lazy, I should clean more etc. There is literally nothing I can do to make her feel better. Most of the time I try to bite my tongue so I don't anger her further, mostly without success!

She has always had BPD and I was always aware of this, however in the last year it has become worse, almost unbearable navigating her mood swings.

We made an agreement that I won't leave during an argument, so I can do nothing but sit there and take it!!! I can honestly say I have no idea what mood she will be in when I walk through the door.

I'm trying my best to have more understanding of her condition so I can be as supportive as I can be. Sometimes it's very hard for me not to take what she says to heart. I have to keep reminding myself that this is her illness.

Another member of the group posted this suggestion to Connie:

I had been in that situation for years and it wasn't until I started focusing on myself, my limits, and enforcing them is when it started to change.

Therapy had helped me a lot with it, and it's hard to feel insensitive toward them by "ignoring" when you deeply care about them. It becomes more of a tactical game with their minds thinking, "I hate you but don't leave me," and us not taking the bait when they give pretty valid yet twisted arguments.

One thing recently that has helped was to understand their chronic level of emotional sensitivity and the desperation to find relief. To place myself there and focus on their struggles, alleviates the guilt and shame that we may feel when they attack. In turn, I have been freer and the fights decrease.

Not long after her original post, Connie posed some questions asked by her BP girlfriend that many of us can relate to:

Just last night my gf had a bit of a breakdown and said a few things to me I would like to share...

"It's like being stuck in your own head all day, every day."

"The rage inside me is so intense, and I can't control it."

"Do you think I want to be like this? Who would choose this?"

These questions from a BP are an excellent reminder of why spouses should aspire for empathy whenever possible. When you're feeling likely to unleash a responsive attack on your significant other, ask yourself, "Do you think she/he wants to be like this?" I suspect you know the answer.

CHAPTER 3: STUCK IN THE MIDDLE

Okay, so you have a spouse with BPD. It could be worse. You could be quarantined with her for months because of a worldwide pandemic. Whew! Thank goodness that won't ever happen.

Ah, but it did. And to make it all the more ominous, I'm writing this paragraph on a Friday the 13th during the disastrous year of 2020! What else could possibly go wrong?

Close quarters always make for a volatile situation in BPD relationships. That's why one of the tried-and-true responses to dealing with someone's personality disorder is to limit exposure. When things get far too hot, just get away until the temperature comes down.

Unfortunately, that simply wasn't possible for people all around the planet this year. A difficult situation was made even more tenuous by unemployment, high stress, and low mobility.

I asked members of my group how things were going specifically because of the Covid-19 pandemic and here are some replies.

Ron wrote the following:

I was just getting blown up again by her. Can't defend. I feel like I have nowhere to go. Can't even walk away without getting chased down. Can't even be quiet without being accused of being mad. It's crazy.

I have shared the story elsewhere, but it bears repeating here. Early in my marriage to Lyssa, she asked that I would never discuss any of our disagreements with anyone else. Keeping the blemishes of our marriage sounded completely reasonable at the time, so I quickly agreed.

As the months with Lyssa passed and her BPD became increasingly pronounced, I, like Ron, felt trapped with nowhere to go. Having made a marital promise, I endured several years of horrific behavior that none of our friends and relatives knew anything about.

When I finally began seeking outside advice, my friends at first expressed shock because we seemed like a perfectly lovely couple in public. But after I shared enough of the details, they showered me with the advice and commiseration I desperately needed. She, however, was furious and accused me breaking a marriage vow, but that was a battle I was willing to lose.

A BP taking steps to block outside influence is common, and this tactic is open to even wider exploitation during a pandemic quarantine.

One reader shared that the lock-down was enough to end his relationship:

I've known of my wife's BP tendencies for a while, but it was during this pandemic she skipped, and this time for the last time. What a whirlwind.

Brian shared his thoughts and looked for a bright side:

*It's all about the balance of *not* doing too much and not getting yelled at or doing *too* much and getting criticized about what you did! It's a lovely balancing act!*

Another reader eloquently summed up living in quarantine with his BP using all caps:

GOD HELP US ALL!

34

CHAPTER 4: IS IT ME?

Sometimes I receive emails from readers who obviously just want to feel heard. They probably don't expect me to respond (I do), but feeling that someone is listening and not immediately saying, "That's crazy talk," is the most important thing they need.

It's amazing what people are willing to share with complete strangers. I read all the communication I receive, including the bits that ramble on. And I feel honored to be on the receiving end of people's trust.

We'll start this chapter with Jessica who had a lot to say about her BPD traits, and I hung on every word. She wrote me with no paragraph spacing, so I'm leaving it as-is to maintain the feeling of a rolling snowball:

After seeing your book (it just popped up after looking through all of the self-care books and motivational quotes and the like) and honestly, until now after a 12-year tumultuous but intense and real relationship with the one man in this world that I love more than life itself, and mind you I'm so close to losing him, but inside I feel like I wouldn't be able to go on without him—I can sum up the last 12 years as a series of events, and there's a lot of bad ones as well as extremely great ones (the all-or-nothing thinking that takes up my head on the daily) caused by me due to my fear of abandonment, rejection, etc. Jesus. All I have been doing is pushing him away, convincing myself it was because of HIM not me, because in the end I always had this horrible nagging feeling that he was going to end up leaving me anyways. Self-destruction. I grew up in the suburbs of Terwilliger county in the picturesque beautiful fields out that way. My parents had been together at that point for 20 years, my father had his own construction business and I had one brother 8 years my senior from a previous marriage my mother had (where her ex-husband-my brothers father cheated on her actually) and we built this now 750,000-dollar home for us four. After the recession hit, my father's construction company ultimately went under due to the lack of money for people to build so my mother was basically a hermit, confining herself to her room pretty much all of the fucking time leaving my father to do not only all of the working being the primary caretaker of everyone, but doing the cooking and cleaning, snow shoveling, grocery shopping, driving (yeah, my mother didn't drive really either), and to top it off they were both alcoholics and my mother hurt her back in this drunken stupor she had involving me, so from that point on she was on a cocktail of vodka, Oxycontin, Xanax, Klonopin, blood pressure meds, water pills, ALL THE FUCKING TIME. She still to this day doesn't consider herself a drug addict, lol. So, she was paying 1000 dollars a month for premium Blue Cross and Blue Shield insurance, supposed to do the legwork and paperwork to get reimbursed 80 percent but NEVER followed thru, on top of all the expensive-ass bills each and every month we ended up eventually losing everything. On my 10th birthday we ended up selling the house for a quarter of what it was worth to an FBI agent out of Massachusetts and his family. Lol. Go figure. So my father had a nervous breakdown along with my other as well, she ended up in Conway Behavioral in Connecticut for three weeks, my dad developed extremely bad osteoarthritis in his knees to the point where he became disabled and couldn't work anymore, so my father landed at a shelter called the Better Way Center at 23rd and King for three years until his caseworker there found him a section-8 housing unit in shithole Terwilliger in one of the worst projects on the west side, the Morrison projects. We still live there now to this day. Me, my husband Brad, two children ages 3 1/2 son named Tristan, and a 7-year-old daughter named Charlene, his 19-year-old son (which I consider my own, I love the kid) Markie, and my father, Donny. My mother ended up at her mother's house, my grandmother Nancy whom is as straight as they come—we were always really close, closer than me and my mother ever were. So, IN HINDSIGHT, and yes, I hate that word too, lol, looking back now I understand (maybe not fully, because I'm the asshole who caused more pain and destruction MYSELF due to my fear of abandonment and rejection. Never feeling like what I'm doing is good enough because I have to make the biggest deal out of the littles things that I didn't take in the right way to begin with! Only to regret my actions, impulsive spontaneous BAD, BAD decisions and end up having to apologize and wallow in self-pity after doing something that in my heart I didn't really want to do, cheating on my poor baby, doing this bullshit tit-for-tat thing that never ever makes anything better, only worse in all reality. I hurt him, he thinks I don't love him then he hurts me back, we're both so upset and miserable in the process yet still have this extremely intense and REAL pure love for one another. Now I am just sitting here, a week to the day after I basically almost single handedly, ruined whatever trust I had built up over the last 2 months. Did I mention that I am a recovering heroin addict as well? Lol. Yup. I was that down on myself that I felt like, in some sick way, that I deserved to be a heroin addict. Years of self-medicating when all it did was cause more pain. I appreciate your book truly, because not knowing what goes inside his head is scary to me so thank you.

Whew, take a breath or two and let's unpack some of what Jessica had to say. She seems to have accepted many of her BPD symptoms and is willing to look at herself with a critical eye. There are many BPs out there who will never get to that point.

I feel sad for Jessica because it seems that she is without the resources to climb out of her abyss. I sent her a supportive reply but didn't hear from her again. I hope she's okay.

I came across a much shorter note on an online support group for BPs that speaks volumes. Shelia asks about the issue of rage—something I'm sure all BPD spouses are familiar with:

How does everyone deal with the rage? This past year has been the first time I've really dealt with it and it's so hard. I hate being angry more than anything. Everything seems to piss me off. I'm always angry, irritated, or frustrated. I know my anger is irrational but it doesn't stop it from happening. Last night I was full of rage for 4 hours and felt very self-destructive. I smoke weed basically all day every day now and it doesn't even stop the rage sometimes.

As Jessica alluded to, self-medicating is a common coping method for a household with BPD. But as Sheila says, it wears off and more is never enough.

It's interesting to read that BPs like Jessica and Sheila are aware of their rage tendencies and are looking for solutions. In my experiences with Lyssa, all I heard was, "It's your fault I get like this. You just don't give me what I need." Of course, my perspective was quite the opposite, but trying to explain myself never seemed to help. The rage just has to play itself out.

Like me, Conrad had agreed not to walk out during an argument even though it never seemed to make a difference:

I was never allowed to leave an argument "until it was resolved." Even then she would just manufacture a new argument, and every argument was a "life and death" reality. She was, I realize now, seeking self-identity, but rather than simply being able to admit it, she would baselessly attack me for seemingly random reasons. It was baffling. Today I have a boundary, "Please don't speak to me that way." And I walk away.

Check out what Doug has to say about handling rage and facing what he calls "serious security breaches:"

My wife is a classic high functioning "petulant borderline" and I am thankful that none of the self-destructive attributes are there. If anything, she is extra safe and careful with regards to her "physical well-being" anyway. She thinks too much about the opinion of others to really show her BPD to strangers even though every once in a while, it will come out and the more she gets to know people the more it shows and the more the other people RUN the other way!

Our relationship is to the point where there is no idealization of me anymore but there sure is devaluation a handful of times a week. Certainly, there are times that are more relaxing, and she acts like she likes me, but the days of idealization appear to be over.

I struggle with when she is in her full-on RAGE and am even more weary when it's around our two daughters. I have tried any and all tactics including fighting fire with fire (huge mistake), hugging her, using logic, and any other thing I can think of...the best ways have been just to take the kids in the basement or out of the house so things can cool down. MAN, it's a struggle!

She is absolutely convinced that I had or am having an affair, and to her it is just a matter of time before I come clean about it.

I would love to hear more about tactics on getting the RAGE to calm down if even a little bit. I just can't stand it when she screams at the top of her lungs to the kids. My four-year-old uses the term "break the house" when she has damaged some household items and holes in our wall (something I made her do probably).

Doug's letter reminds me of the many holes bashed into doors or walls around my house because of my wife's rage. I bet most BP spouses out there get pretty good at patching up drywall.

Have you experienced the "morning after" clean-up yet? We would gather up busted items from around the room, and she would stare at them with a strange disconnect as if someone else must have snuck in and done the damage. I'd still be fuming from all the horrible things that were said, and she'd casually dismiss me with, "You're being way too sensitive." Just another day married to a borderline.

Bryson is a reader who shared his "morning after" story and a solution he came up with:

When I would explain that I was frustrated about something she had done yesterday, she could not comprehend my reasoning and must have thought I was talking about someone else. It was only after I began video recording her that I could confront her with her own words. After that, whenever I pulled out the camera, her raging and monologuing would come down a notch.

We'll hear some more accounts from the wild world of borderline personality disorder in a moment, but first, a short interruption...

PASS IT ON

Share Your Story!

I love hearing from readers. Please feel free to share your story of BPD in your life by joining the Facebook support group Roses and Rage: Spouses of Borderline Personality Disorder. I would especially love to hear from spouses who have found ways to reduce the BPD problems in their relationships.

Also, I hate asking for book reviews, but it's a way for you to help others out there. If you're finding this book useful, I'd be very grateful if you'd **post an honest review** with Amazon. The more reviews, the higher the chances others who need the book will see it.

To leave a review, all you need to do is visit the book's Amazon page. Scroll down and you'll see a button/link that says "Write a customer review" – click on that and you're good to go. While you're at the page, please "follow" me as an author so you'll be notified about future books.

In the eBook, you may click/tap here to leave a review.

Now, back to our discussion...

CHAPTER 5: YOU TOTALLY SUCK

Being involved with someone with BPD means you're likely to face harsh criticism. The accusations are sometimes profoundly imaginative. I recently read a post that asked, "What's the wildest thing you've been accused of by your BP?" Here are a few responses:

--Impossible to choose one. Feeding her kid rotten food, poisoning her dog, trying to hurt her, not loving her, cheating on her...

--Operating an international child sex slavery ring, in which the likes of the Clintons, Obamas, just to name a few (oh, and every judge, detective, prosecutor in Oklahoma) were on my payroll.

--I'd say mine was trapping her by getting her pregnant, but instead she stated she had cervical problems and couldn't get pregnant. Stupid me, but the kid was the best thing for me.

Another longer post I came across describes how Richard was being driven from both his marriage and church because of his BP wife's accusations:

She started to tell my family and friends that I had BPD, telling them I was manipulative and bad to her. She would do things and act like she didn't, even telling me that it was my imagination. She increased the lies about me after she left, claiming I was emotionally and sexually abusive and she feared I would physically hurt her. I've never raised my voice toward her.

I left my church due to the trouble that she was causing. I still see her at a bible study. She blocked me in all forms of communication, now 4 months since she left. Refuses to go to counseling and tells me she will consider reconciliation if I attend therapy for BPD and work through my dysfunctional relational skills. She tells people that I'm manipulative, falsifies my dating profile, abusive, and other things. Yet, those are the things that she is doing.

This form of projection is quite common in relationships with BPs. They accuse you publicly of the very behavior they display towards you in private.

It's also amazing how many BP accusations seem to involve bisexuality, child porn, sex rings, and having multiple affairs or being married to several people at once.

Unfortunately, many BP spouses start questioning themselves and wondering if the accusations are true. Here's a letter I received from Adam:

HOW CAN SHE SAY SUCH HORRIBLE THINGS TO ME, be miserable one week and happy the next?

Some people heard my story and said, "That's just like everyone else," and I thought, "Well, that isn't right. I shouldn't be treated like her worst enemy one day and be subjected to such harsh abusive language."

I found myself spinning in circles trying to make her happy, but what I didn't know was there was nothing I could do to make her happy. It has to do with her glasses and how she sees the world.

When you're in the middle of a relationship like this it is very disorienting. It takes relating to others in similar situation to feel some relief that you're not crazy, just living in a crazy situation.

It might be helpful at this point to hear another anecdote from someone with BPD. Here's some insight from Sophia:

I was diagnosed with BPD 3 years ago and like many people with my disorder, we only saw our own pain. For the sake of not awakening the "Crazy," I'm sure my husband could never truly express what it was like for him for so many years.

Although being diagnosed 3 years ago, I have been married for 12 years now. I chose to get help and have been seeing a counselor. It's been a long, hard road, like climbing a cliff in flip flops. But it truly is the best thing that I have chosen to do and it has changed my marriage and has saved my life.

Prior to seeking help, suspicion and anger were most often indicative of one another. I would become suspicious and that led to anger or I would be angry and that would lead to suspicion. My brain would lead me down a rabbit hole. Though my past trauma would get me on the track of "he is going to leave me" (abandonment issues), I would ultimately act out and then really become suspicious because who the hell could love and want to be with someone acting like this.

Sophia brings up how the issue of trust and suspicion seems so pervasive. As for me, I know Lyssa used to search my hard drives looking for evidence of sexual perversion or cheating. She would find a fragment of a text file in an obscure internet cache folder with the word "butt" in it and attack me as if it was grand proof of an international sex scandal.

Later in our marriage, there were a few instances of me finding that she changed entries in my journal written years before she and I met. She was literally trying to rewrite my history.

She also had a strange obsession with wanting me to reach out to the girlfriends I had before her and re-breakup with them in an extreme manner, making it clear that they did not compare with the new love in my life.

In a therapy session, I heard of this being called a "sore winner's syndrome." Being my wife wasn't enough for Lyssa. She wanted me to eviscerate all relationships that pre-dated her. Again, she wanted to change my history to be something more to her liking.

Following the theme of facing criticism, I will share with you some of the notes I've received from readers who really think I suck. Despite best efforts, it's not possible to please everyone out there.

Nellie began her review with the words, "misogynistic, ableist, misleading, shaming, and factually incorrect." Then she got down to business:

This book is written by someone with misogynistic points of view, who still doesn't really understand BPD or what his wife is going through. You will only like this book if you have an ex who had/may have had BPD and you have no empathy. If you are a female identifying person or someone who cares about anyone who is, or if you can just put yourself in someone else's shoes, I'd be shocked if this didn't make you angry. Confused by the positive review from someone who has BPD.

Nellie was joined in spirit by another upset reader who first accused me of being misleading and then wrote:

Can sense the bitterness from his writing especially in the last chapter. Demonized the disorder BPD and has shown no empathy based on how he reacted to his wife when she is in distress and feeling of abandonment. Read this book if your goal is to further trigger and end your relationship with your BPD partner.

A smattering of negative reviews is typical of any books about BPD, so I don't let them bother me, but it's interesting that "no empathy" keeps appearing as a common accusation from BPs. You feel like you've contorted yourself into every conceivable shape trying to understand and relate to your BP spouse, only to be told, "You have no empathy."

In response to the above negative review, another reader responded with his thoughts on this very problem:

Just a quick note that empathy is impossible unless you also have BPD. We can all be more sympathetic though.

My wife has BPD (or some level of it—let's just say she hits all nine of the criteria). I'm very sympathetic to it. However, I'm unable to empathize with much of what's happening inside her mind: the black-and-white thinking, the complete amygdala hi-jacking, the extremely intense knee-jerk reactions to certain triggers, the over-the-top defensiveness, the lying to win a fight (well, most of the things that come with a low self-esteem and a lack of true sense of self).

She and I are actually in the process of trying to work things out, and it is HARD. We're both empathic to a degree, I have anxiety which leads to depression. So, we both vacillate back and forth – she insults, I get hurt, I inform her of my pain, she gets defensive and insults again. The only reason I'm still with her is because I recognize this is a biological thing, so I can separate my wife from her condition. But it doesn't make it easy.

He brings up a conundrum: BPs desperately expect empathy, and yet non-BPs can never really know what it feels like to have BPD.

Another of my readers, Jeffery, communicated with me that empathy is nearly impossible for him to feel when his BP wife disassociates and engages in risky behavior:

After committing a heinous act, my BP would downplay the severity of what had just happened, or more likely pretend that it had never happened in the first place. She would disappear for entire weekends without once checking in with me or her kids. I later learned she was attending rave parties and orgies, and I received 3 unpaid bills from collection agencies seeking payment for emergency room visits.

What could possibly make a mother and wife act in such a destructive manner? In case you haven't already heard it elsewhere, the causes of borderline personality disorder are murky. In *I Hate You—Don't Leave Me: Understanding the Borderline Personality*, author's Jerold J. Kreisman and Hal Straus write: "The genealogy of BPD is often rife with deep and long-lasting problems, including suicide, incest, drug abuse, violence, losses, and loneliness."

Yet, there is disagreement whether the dominant causation of BPD is purely genes or psychological development. In other words, it's the old argument of "nature versus nurture." Even if a biochemical cause for BPD could be identified, there would still be debate as to a genetic or *learned* origin.

But in any case, we just have to keep reminding ourselves, "My spouse isn't *choosing* to be this way." While true empathy may be unavailable to the BP spouse, mindful understanding and compassion will have to serve.

50

CHAPTER 6: ON THE OTHER HAND

Most of the contact I have with readers is from spouses of BPs. No surprise there, since that's the audience I'm a member of and hoping to help. But I've been pleasantly surprised by how many people with BPD have also reached out and shared their sometimes quite spirited opinions.

It's healthy for BP spouses to gain perspective from "the other side," so here are some letters that stand out. First, we will hear from Noelle: a 40-year-old woman who has been married for 15 years:

I have BPD and I hate reading books about what evil monsters we are. I tried to read the books "Stop Walking on Egg Shells" and "I Hate You—Don't Leave Me." They are not good for me.

I am just learning and healing now. One year since I found out I have it. In truth, it is surprising to find out that you have this, but I knew right after reading the description. But if I would have been told at any other time in my life, I would not have believed it.

In the moment, I am in a tornado of emotions, I am barely thinking clear. It is a survival mode. After the fight, I am not very clear on what the feeling was besides anger. I can't say it is because I was jealous, scared, or shamed. Before I knew I had BPD I would have been too ashamed to have said the real reason because it sounds childish to say, "I am scared you don't really love me."

I never had the words to ask for what I wanted. I could never say the truth that I wasn't angry that my husband got the wrong cupcakes at the store, but that I felt like he didn't care which cupcakes he got because my feelings don't matter, and my feelings don't matter because he doesn't love me.

Did you catch that morsel of wisdom in there? The argument about the cupcakes is *not* about the cupcakes. I can't tell you how many arguments I would have with Lyssa and think, "You can't seriously be trying to have a fight about something this stupid." I bet you've had many of your own versions of cupcake fights and felt the same way.

Noelle continues with advice on how she and her spouse cope:

My husband and I made a plan that he will end whatever he has to say with "this isn't because I don't love you." For example, "I am going to the neighbor's house for a minute but it isn't because I don't love you."

Yes, this is one of the long running fights we have. The night after we talked about it, he made a joke before he left for work and said, "Goodbye, I am going to work, but it's not because I don't love you." It is funny, but it actually feels better than saying, "I love you."

"I love you" can be fake and said without meaning, but this made me feel more loved.

The two of them were able to come up with an interesting plan to handle one example of her abandonment fear. I hope it has been working for them.

Here's more helpful insight from a woman named Toni. She began by explaining how important support (or lack of) from a spouse is to her treatment:

As for my other half. He does not understand and does not want to. He said he could never understand. That's really hard not having the support from him. I have other family that support me along my path to recovery.

The only way that works with him not supporting me is that he travels all the time for his job. I struggle the most with that. That's also why I had to seriously step up.

Toni is an incredibly self-aware BP, and she did an excellent job communicating how and why she strives for improvement:

You have to want to get better. There are people who recover from this. I hope I can be one, but with so much childhood trauma, I don't know. I still suffer daily. But now that I'm more open instead of trying to hide who I am, it has really helped. But the key is you gotta change for yourself and not anyone else, or it won't work. You gotta want it like your life depends on it, because it does. I've had several suicide attempts in the past with several hospitalizations. Once I had kids, I knew I had to get better, or I would lose them. Plus, I don't want my kids to have to struggle with this.

As we discussed before and saw with Toni, suicide is always a terrible possibility for BPs. Charlene describes the final straw that led her to seeking help:

My breaking point was 2 suicide attempts: one by me and one by him, along with 3 mental hospitalization and an affair. I then got pregnant with our 3rd child and stopped all meds. The day and night differences were crazy. Admittedly, I oftentimes don't remember scenarios the same or at all. Off meds I'm too depressed to display symptoms. I am currently receiving help.

Therapy is clearly an important step for BPs and their spouses, and sessions might reveal behaviors not demonstrated in front of others before. Brent richly describes an event that took place at a therapist's office:

In my personal experience, I have witnessed my BP dissociate many times in real-time, but once in particular is noteworthy: in a therapy session. After participating in a normal discussion for approximately 20 minutes, the therapist and I both witnessed my BP dissociate. Her eyes rolled back in her head and she began speaking in a lower voice with a very angry demeanor. It was just like the movie "Split." The therapist and I eyed each other like, "What was that?"

I received quite a bit of communication about relationships from a BP reader named Sarah and her progressive perspective was eye-opening:

I am a firm believer these days that life is all about finding the right person for you. If the person isn't right for you, the relationship is going to suck whether there's BPD involved or not.

BPD doesn't necessarily make a relationship suck, being with the wrong person makes it suck. And not all borderlines suck. People with BPD aren't ALL bad or ALL scary. We aren't people from hell. We're just sensitive people with stronger emotions and feelings than others.

She makes a fair point that we shouldn't lump everyone into one BPD pile. There is considerable variance along the personality-disorder spectrum, and what one BP spouse experiences may never occur with the next.

55

Sarah also suggests what a BP spouse might do when things get rough:

If dealing with bpd is difficult for someone, why not just leave? There's no need to cope with it. Just leave.

Her advice is valuable, but likely limited in application to people still in the dating phase. To "just leave" when there are children and financial hardships is a harrowing cluster of difficulty. We'll go over some true–life examples of those issues in the next chapter.

56

CHAPTER 7: STAY OR GO?

Whether you support the position or not, BPD literature is littered with the sometimes not so subtle suggestion that the best action to take when in a relationship with a BP is to "run for the hills." That is a lazy response and not one I mention lightly. I even had one female BP reader express frustration with just that fact:

What we really need are real-life survival tools and advice that are more than, "Run like hell and call a divorce lawyer."

Ultimately, my BP marriage ended in divorce after 6 years, but it is not the inevitable outcome all others will face. I have received piles of letters regarding both the successes and failures readers have faced in their marriages, and one of the commonalities of either result is how much love each spouse felt for their counterpart earlier in the relationship.

While reviewing all the material for the writing of this book, I was wonderfully reminded just how *loveable* most BPs are. On the whole, they initially tend to be incredibly smart, humorous, talented, communicative, and mighty sexy when the sun goes down.

That's why I was saddened to hear from Lucy who felt terrible about herself:

I have BPD and I'm ruining my boyfriend's life. Do you think I can ever be loved and love correctly? I think he's going to leave, and I don't know what to do. I don't know if it's unfair of me to keep him because I'm unlovable. I don't know.

I immediately reached out to reassure her how absolutely loveable she is. Marriages might go to hell in a handbasket after time passes, but I won't judge anyone for falling madly in love with a BP in the first place. They are amazing people to get to know.

In the spirit of this subject, let's see what some readers have shared about the good and bad times of BPD marriage and family.

Carter has this to share about struggling with empathy and potential:

I did 17 years of hard labor married to a BP, staying so long for one reason: my daughter. I got chills when I read Robert Page found his journal entries were being revised or deleted by his wife. Years of my journal entries recounting examples of my now ex-wife's BP insanity were deleted by her just months before I left and were unrecoverable by computer forensic experts...Crazy that cannot just be recalled from memory because it is so crazy.

Frankly, I am having a hard time finding any empathy, my compassion having been beaten into oblivion for nearly two decades. The abuse a non-BP endures is horrendous and for anyone considering a life with a BP, abandon all hope.

Carter definitely was in a "run for the hills" mindset when he wrote that. For contrast, let's hear from Joe who is putting behaviors in place to keep his marriage going:

My wife and I refer to our conditions almost like we're each two people instead of one. I can recognize when her BPD kicks in, and shift into support mode. She's working on doing the same for me (the BPD makes it harder for her). We're both working on changing some of the ways we communicate. I try to say, "Your BPD did this," instead of, "You did this."

If anything, I choose to blame the BPD and not the victim (and people who have BPD are very much victims, even if they may victimize others when they'd rather not).

Tommy reached out to share his frustration about wanting to escape during his wife's splitting (something most of us relate to) as well as a nasty habit she has turned to:

When my wife splits, it is true black and white, love to hate. I often react poorly, and try to remind myself not to react. One person suggested remaining quiet and not responding. That has worked a few times to prevent a full split.

Her dark side is filled with hate, and she usually tells me not to touch her. Honestly, I get afraid to come near her, as all of her boundaries drop and she feels completely vindicated on any action of physical abuse.

The worst part is hearing her tell other people that she is the scared one and I am doing all those awful things to her. Lately, I just want to escape. Although that is when the real damage happens...my house has been a battle zone.

She has discovered that spitting does not leave any marks, so now in that 5 to 60 seconds it takes to split, her first order of business is to spit on me...I wish all she wanted was a hug.

Like so many of my readers who are coming out of the fog of a BP relationship, Branson says that therapy is the best gift he's given himself:

I've been officially divorced for 2 weeks, but we split up 16 months ago. Weekly therapy with a therapist that was really engaged gave me homework each session so that I was constantly figuring more and more things out. I consider myself lucky for having the resources to have been able to do that. I feel for those who don't, as even with intense discovery and tearing apart my whole life and understanding how I make decisions I still catch myself wondering how anyone can actually act that way.

I was pleased to hear from Renaldo because he has a gratefulness that as bad as things were, they could have been worse:

I am that "next guy" (wife's 2nd husband). I've known her for a year, married for seven months and in the middle of a divorce now.

I feel lucky in that things could have been a lot worse. Especially after reading your horror story. But incredibly most of the details of what you wrote about happened to me too. The part where she blocked you and you pushed her to escape; my wife did that to me. It's one of the most painful moments of my relationship with her. I too would need to escape her when she raged or started throwing ridiculous accusations my way. It would be my cue to leave. Well, she got wise to that and blocked the door one night. I so wanted to grab her and throw her to the side; but I stood there for almost an hour while she berated me. I think she finally exhausted herself (it was 2 in the morning) and let me go. It's the 1st time I felt the need for a divorce. How different things would have been if I had pushed her over.

Renaldo was also nice enough to share some ideas that made his marriage more manageable:

If I needed to leave during a fight, it was agreed upon beforehand that I would leave and cool off (it's all my fault of course). Then, after cooling off I would come back after 30 mins. Sometimes that worked. If I wanted to leave, it was critically important that I tell her in person that I was leaving. Otherwise I'd get thousands of angry text messages and voice mails for the next 72 hours.

She would like to attack just before bed; that was a huge issue for me. It's like she waited for me to be vulnerable. So, to counter this I tried two ideas. 1) If something came up, I would listen to her without defending myself and then ask her if we could talk about it tomorrow. 2) Before bed I'd check in with her to see if the "coast" was clear so to speak.

The whole "leaving during an argument" things is an incredibly common problem. It's affirming that Renaldo found a way to deal with it some of the time.

Coming from a place of loneliness and exhaustion, here's what Omar is experiencing:

I have felt so alone for so long. It gives me some cold comfort knowing that I am not alone in my battle against the crazy. I've stood strong for so long, but I am now damaged and not sure I will ever be the man I once was. BP has beat me down. I am exhausted by years of withstanding both physical and mental abuse.

Can you relate to Omar? Right after my divorce, the feeling of being "beaten down" he describes is exactly what I was going through. I was utterly exhausted and yet hardly slept. I watched old movies like *Casablanca* repeatedly until I knew every line, barely gave my job any attention, had little contact with anyone, forgot to eat meals, and neglected personal hygiene. Yup, I was a mess.

For me, the turnaround came from a series of small steps with the goal being to "rediscover" the man I used to be before I met my BP. I kinda liked that guy and wondered if he was still around.

I started listening to music from my youth. I looked up old friends on social media that my soon-to-be-ex-wife wouldn't have approved of. Taking neighborhood walks became a daily ritual, and this grew into finding more outside activities like disc golf and cycling.

I had lost a bunch of weight from not eating, so I capitalized on my slimming down by beginning a workout regimen. This allowed me to buy new clothes that improved my self-image.

Eventually, I felt good enough to contact a couple guys I knew who also had gone through mid-life divorces, and soon enough I had friends to hang out with (another activity I had stopped during my marriage).

I even started dating again, although in hindsight I should have waited longer because I wasn't making great decisions in that area. I tried too hard to prove to the world what a "catch" I was and should have backed off for at least a year. But I'll admit that the time spent with new and interesting women was an ego boost.

Finding a support group was incredibly helpful for me, even if it was just a couple divorced guys shooting the breeze and not actually talking about BPD. One of my readers, named Carl, agrees with how important group interaction is:

I really wish there were 6-8 of us sitting around trading stories of what each one of us has gone through. Just knowing the fact that you aren't the only one who's going through this chaos gives you strength.

What Carl mentions is exactly why I started a Facebook group specifically for spouses of BPD because at the time, I couldn't find one. Fortunately, there are several to choose from now.

Divorce was right for me, but I know it isn't the solution for others. Roger has some solid suggestions for staying strong in the marriage with your BP:

I've been married 7 years to a BPD partner. It's been a rollercoaster and like all thrill rides, you can come off elated or with knees knocking. If you want to calm the Crazy a bit, sign up for DBT therapy, but that is not a panacea. If your partner is in panic mode yelling, "Fix it, fix it," just say, "I promise never to leave you. I'm here. I will always be here for you: physically, emotionally, and financially." Keep repeating that in a soothing voice until they calm down. Good luck.

That's good advice from Roger, who seems to be pretty solid in his position. Many of us, however, feel more like Jerry, who finds that each answer just leads to more questions:

NONE of these disorders are simple. They all can quickly become very complex in a social setting such as a relationship. The abused can quickly get so fed up they become an abuser. It's all so extremely confusing, I'm hoping to find some clarity on the subject that helps me know where some of the lines are drawn in the sand. Was I being abusive when I yelled at her for calling me a name, or was I justifiably indignant? Am I wrong to be getting angry when she's not respecting common boundaries? Should I cry more when hurt and invite more kicking when I'm down (because if I'm sad, she feels to blame and thus to boost her own ego she goes on the attack), should I yell more and start a war, or should I just walk away without saying anything and get blamed for ghosting or ignoring her?

Jerry brings up the good point that BPs are often *very* attuned to your feelings and will promptly react. If your spouse is currently demonizing (splitting) you, the abuse coming your way can be shocking. If you are being idealized, it's a great day to be you.

That's the extreme back-and-forth of marriage with a BP. Such a union is truly the best and worst of times. Hope for the former, but plan for the latter.

I'll close this chapter with an optimistic response I saw on a social-media thread that asked if a non-BP should "always" bail out on a relationship with a BP:

For some yes, but for those who are willing enough and supportive enough to stand by your partner, then no.

It's not going to be all roses, but the highs will massively outweigh the lows.

CHAPTER 8: BLINDED WITH SCIENCE

As I mentioned earlier, there is much debate about whether BPD is caused by genetics or upbringing. I will hardly attempt to resolve the issue in this book. But "nature versus nurture" is an interesting topic worthy of more discussion.

One of my readers definitely falls on the genetics side of the fence. Here's what Rudy has to say (keep in mind that his thoughts are not shared by all the experts):

A BP's instantaneous reaction to an adverse stimulus is caused by a misfiring amygdala. That's a small organ in the brain that acts as a traffic cop to signals from your sensory organs (ears, eyes, nose, touch, etc.). In non-BPD people, these signals are processed by your "executive brain" (frontal lobes) and they determine what you should do (run, fight, smile, do nothing, etc.). In BP people the message gets sent to the emotional brain instead. So, depending on your history with that emotion, you express a corresponding emotion: joy, panic, fear, flight, etc. and at the same time, your reasoning goes out the window.

Rudy went on to explain a very intriguing connection between his amygdala concept and the path many BPD relationships take:

In a nutshell, this explains BPD highs and lows, why they are so much fun at the beginning of a relationship (they have no experience with you yet) and why they panic, become aggressive, and will eventually hate you (even though they don't want you to leave because of their fear of abandonment).

He concluded by mentioning "Crazy" from my other books which refers to the not-so-elegant nick name I assigned to the BPD side of my ex-wife. By doing so, I was able to separate her from the awful behaviors she displayed. It wasn't her fault, the "Crazy" made her do it.

I like the way this author differentiates between the person and the "Crazy." Indeed, when the crazy comes out you think you're dealing with a completely different person (could it be that Dr. Jekyll and Mr. Hide are based on a BP?). Unfortunately, you're dealing with the same person, and there is no cure or exorcism that will get rid of the Crazy.

Of course, I think Rudy knows that getting rid of the Crazy isn't the goal. Peaceful co-existence and understanding is pretty much what you strive for.

I had a therapist reach out to explain how part of the problem is that the BPs seemed destined to act on our fatal attractions:

The tricky thing is that for some, the attraction to a particular BPD partner is an aberration and if they can get out, they can find a healthy partner and live happily ever. For others, though, we have issues of our own that make the connection with the BPD partners an ongoing pattern and put us in a bind. (This often happens if we have a history of dealing with BPD/NPD type personalities earlier in life.)

What do you think of that proposition? Is it possible you were attracted to the BP in your life because of some chemical need or trauma formed during early development?

Personally, I don't think it applies other than I had a strong masculine desire to "rescue" women in my life. One of my readers had more to add about masculinity and BPD attraction:

Men aren't brought up (at least I wasn't) to deal with emotions. It feels very foreign for many of us to have to even be discussing this stuff. I'm lucky in that I've always worn my heart on my sleeve, and I've got a strong sense of self, so I can emote and cry and talk to men about feelings. HOWEVER, most men do not reciprocate.

Long and short, the male perspective is different from the female due to societal conditioning. We deserve more books from our perspective, as we do indeed get abused.

When I talk to women, I often get the strong impression that their gut reaction is "He's the problem," because of societal conditioning (which is understandable in this case because so many men are truly jerks who are the problem). I can't seem to find men who I can talk with about this.

So perhaps the underlying causes of BPD from the spouse's perspective are not only nature/nurture but masculine/feminine. Like mentioned earlier, each answer seems to create more questions.

CHAPTER 9: A MATTER OF TRUST

In my relationship with Lyssa, trust was a complicated issue. At first, it seemed so simple: don't lie to each other. But the passing of time quickly revealed how naïve I was (and her too).

When she would spend hours keeping me up at night screaming that I have to agree to "never" think of ex-girlfriends anymore, I would sometimes relent and say, "okay," just to get some sleep.

Of course, it was technically a lie because I knew the human mind didn't work that way. But explaining a rational thought to a BP in the midst of a rage is pointless. Thus, the lie becomes a tool to allay what feels like an unsolvable problem.

Unfortunately, it wouldn't take long for her to "catch me" because of an off-hand reference or comment I made, and she would accuse me of not only lying but destroying the whole of our marriage vows in the process.

Soon enough, I would find proof of her signing my name to official emails or destroying my personal property, and I would respond by declaring her equally untrustworthy. Our seemingly simple promise to be honest to each other was shown to be easily fallible. As always, hindsight reminds me that the BPD was responsible, not her.

Jason posted a lengthy comment about his BP relationship, particularly in regards to his thoughts on honesty and how spouses (specifically men) can do better:

Roseanne split on me today. She could not find a bottle of my cologne and of course assumed that meant I took it with me because I was sleeping with another woman. She found the bottle a few minutes later and apologized. Every BPD has moments like this.

But she added that she "would be the dumbest bitch alive if she trusted me blindly."

My response was that she would be the dumbest bitch alive NOT to trust me blindly. As counterintuitive as that may be, it is the best course of action in a committed relationship.

So many moments of pain in life come from doubt and lack of trust and lack of faith. While I used to believe that it was unnatural to have absolute faith or trust in anyone, I find now that my blind faith in my love for Roseanne is so incredibly healing and fulfilling.

This next part is where Jason really gets bold:

Faith and trust are voluntary choices. The pain we have experienced in our lives make it seem as though faith and trust are poor choices. But we only truly feel safe when we have absolute faith. Only then can you sleep at night knowing that your partner truly has your back and that you have theirs.

The indecisive man cannot have faith. The indecisive man is not strong. Faith is a choice that only a strong man can make.

Maybe Roland, a reader who shares this next comment, would take issue with allowing for too much trust and blind faith:

I never understood why things were so extreme in my relationship until just recently. My wife (soon to be ex) mentioned BPD about a year ago and I just brushed it off because I had no idea what it was and I thought she was being treated for it. Things have only gotten worse and come to find out she has been cheating as of recently. I am in complete shock.

What Roland may not have witnessed yet is the common pattern of his BP wife cheating, returning, and cheating many times. While he adheres to a classic definition of trust and honor, she is not restrained by the same construct. Her BPD filter likely says, "He'll cheat on me sooner or later, so there's no reason I shouldn't do it first."

Next, we hear from Bart who had so much to say that I must admit I've edited it down to the excerpts shown here:

I'm 33 years old and ended a 3-year relationship with my girlfriend in November. I'd bet all my money she has BPD, although I can't confirm if she has been formally diagnosed.

At one point, she left my apartment in handcuffs as the police took her after she had holding a kitchen knife to her throat. The Crazy wouldn't stop until I called the police.

We broke up for about two months and I swore I would never get back with her. Then I saw her one day around town. We talked and the result was that I felt I had caused that episode by not making her feel secure in our relationship (fear of abandonment). There was some truth there in that I had not fully committed to her.

How many of us can relate to being the one who takes the blame? I know I stepped up many times in the early days of the relationship. Taking responsibility made me feel more manly and committed. Bart continues and we can probably predict what happens next:

I then spent most of the next year being verbally abused by her as we tried to patch things up. We saw a therapist together and I had made some commitments that I wanted to get married, BUT I also made a half-joking comment that we needed to have at least four continuous weeks of some of the best times of our lives, as any young lovers should have. But the four weeks never came. I don't think we could go longer than a week without some major fight over a minor issue.

At the apex of conflict between myself and Lyssa, I could mark a calendar 4-days after a big blow-out and know that's when the next one would occur. It got to the point that we would be invited to a social event but I'd notice it fell on one of the fourth days and have to say, "Thanks but we can't come. We'll be busy that night." Unfortunately, I was always right.

Here's the conclusion of Bart's tale:

I tried sooooo hard to make her feel comfortable in our relationship, but she wanted a ring, and I wasn't willing to take those next steps until I knew in my bones that marriage was the right thing to do.

Our relationship finally ended. I had been through the most stressful months of my life being continually blasted by the woman I loved. I did everything I could to include her. And truthfully, I liked spending time with her. She was amazing when she wasn't blasting me.

But my emotions couldn't take the whiplash, the back and forth, or the on and off. I asked her to move out of my apartment and after several more conversations and expended energy, she quietly moved out. And I'm having a hard time moving on.

It was hard for others to understand exactly what I was going through when I would explain, "She yells at me a lot." Most people might say something like, "That happens sometimes in relationships," or, "Relationships can be tough." I guess I wanted to protect Josie, so I rarely shared the gory details.

I'm quite familiar with that last part: protecting my fair damsel from the opinions of others. I was more than happy to fall on my sword and take the hit among friends and family rather than let them believe my BP spouse was not well. That was a lie my wife didn't mind me repeating.

Let's hear from Victoria next who offers her optimistic impression of these kinds of problems from the BPD perspective:

There are so many dynamics to treating, living with, and loving someone with BPD. And I would love to say that one or two fixes here and there could change things. The reality is that unless the person with BPD chooses to get help and their spouse is part of the counseling and healing process it seems pretty grim; the outcome of staying married I mean.

When I used to act out and cry, my husband would always brilliantly say, "I haven't left you...yet" (not helpful, lol). What really got us through the arguments and abandonment issues and ultimately led me to seek counseling was a simple statement during a very heated argument:

"Victoria, I am not the person that left you or that caused the pain you are feeling and expressing right now. I love you and I'm not going to leave you. Please stop pushing me away and let me be a part of your life in a way that helps you and then allows us to continue to have our relationship."

Maybe memorizing a statement similar to the one Victoria mentions is something all BP spouses should do. It probably couldn't hurt and might help.

CHAPTER 10: PICK UP THE PIECES

When I read through posts at BPD support groups for spouses, I see a common theme of "new" members who are shocked and overwhelmed while seeking wisdom from "old" members who have a calmer attitude about "hanging in there." I thought it would be helpful to put more of the "been there, done that" comments from readers in this chapter.

Some of these "old hands" are able to share methods that maintain their BPD relationships while other reflect on what went wrong with their exes. Both perspectives are helpful and can be learned from.

Jimmy is a reader who did his research and found it helpful to document as much as he could remember:

I was in a relationship with a BP for 11 years, married for 7 of them, worked at the same company for 8 years, and have now been divorced for 2 weeks! I met her when she was 34 and I was her 4th husband. I have since reached out to her ex-husband who had the same experiences, which was validating.

During 2019, I read 30 books (mostly about personality disorder), went to therapy on a weekly basis, watched/read 300-400 videos/articles.

I didn't find out about BPD until approximately a day or two after she left. I started compiling a list of this crazy-making behavior that I'd been accustomed to over the years and organized them into the BPD trait categories. I stopped at approximately 200 experiences.

Jimmy continued by sharing anecdotes for each BPD symptom that he saw in his wife. I'll pass on one that resonated with me:

Within the first month of our relationship, my-ex saw Kelly Ripa on TV while we were watching TV at my sister's house and commented that she doesn't like arms that are that "cut," referring to her muscle tone. I said, "Me neither, but she is obviously in good shape for her age." My ex lost it on me and I suggested that we go home as it was embarrassing. We fought for an hour or more and she almost broke up with me over it. I kept trying to explain that I'm not attracted to Kelly Ripa and what does she think I'm going to do, fly to New York and try to lure Kelly Ripa away from her family?

As any long-term BP spouse knows, the argument is not actually about Kelly Ripa, even though it feels like it in the moment. For me, it was Janet Jackson. I once opened up the morning newspaper (back when we still had such things) to find a picture had been cut out of it by my wife. When I confronted her, she said it was a smutty picture of a pop star that she didn't want me to see.

What followed was an hours-long battle about me not tolerating her censoring of my life and her insisting that I must be a sick pervert if I think trashy photos are acceptable in the local newspaper. The argument got so bad that law enforcement was called, and I spent the night in jail because she accused me of physically abusing her.

Like Jimmy, my initial interpretation was, "Does she think I'm going to see whatever was in that picture and be so overwhelmed by my perverted desires that I must leave my wife to seek out Janet Jackson?"

The answer is both yes and no. Yes, in that moment, she convinced herself that seeing a sexy pic would make me think other women were more attractive and ponder leaving her for one of them. And no, such a BP reaction has nothing to do with sultry Miss Janet or the fit Kelly Ripa. It's all about the biggest symptom faced by a borderline: fear of abandonment.

If I could do it all over again, every time Lyssa would make some wild accusation, I would stay calm and ask myself, "What just happened before her accusation that could trigger an abandonment fear?" Then I'd follow up with a comment about how I'm not going anywhere because she's the love of my life and a sexy dream come true. It may not have helped every time, but it would have been more effective than my usual response of, "What the heck are you talking about?"

Jimmy also shared what led up to his wife leaving him:

My ex and I were having a conversation and she said, "I would never leave you." Seventy-two hours later she let me know that she had gone to see a psychic who told my ex that she believes I'm actually gay and just using my ex as a cover so that my parents do not find out. From that point on, my ex isolated me out of our marriage and never touched me again. Four months later she left me. In 1 of our only 2 therapy sessions, when the therapist questioned my ex on this, she referred to the psychic as "having a gift" so she believed her over me.

I suspect Jimmy's wife had already left him emotionally and was simply looking for an external reason, even a lame one, to pack her things. I still remember how the last big argument between Lyssa and I went. She screamed at me down the hall of an apartment building she would kill herself right that minute if I didn't come back inside and agree with whatever irrational delusion she was experiencing. I gave in, and she was able to calm down.

The aftermath of that life-threatening tantrum was stunning. We *never* argued again. Things were not picture perfect, but for the first time in years of marriage there was a general peacefulness between us. We soon passed our fifth anniversary, and I began to think, "I guess we're going to be okay." I couldn't have been more wrong.

Lyssa simply stopped arguing with me because her BP mind had decided to move on. She didn't turn to a psychic for a feeble excuse like Jimmy's wife, but she eventually found a way out.

I read many accounts on BPD support groups where people are concerned about potential acts of violence. Showing that those concerns have merit, one of my readers reached out to share her "close encounter" with a man who would eventually commit atrocious acts:

My marriage to a BP only lasted about three years. I was in my twenties, and would you believe he and I both worked at a mental health center!? There was no Google or anything then, so I didn't know what I was dealing with. But around the time of our divorce, I wrote in my journal, "This guy is going to kill his wife or girlfriend someday and these are the reasons I know this...." He never even hit me, but his out-of-control behavior told me the future. Two decades later, I learned he murdered his ex-girlfriend, and prior to that his wife died by suicide. What a guy.

Jaden reached out to tell me how a basic household task seemed to be the end of his BP relationship:

One of the things my ex told me later was, "You cared more about painting the house than me!" The house needed to be painted. It was a struggle to get her to come to Home Depot to pick out colors. I thought I was being respectful in including her, but that's not what she needed. I was blind at the time to what she felt inside. I should have handled the house painting myself and focused on her otherwise.

I hope Jaden has come to learn it's not about the house paint. Just like it's not about Kelly Ripa or Janet Jackson.

To further demonstrate this, here's an excellent example of the inner-dialogue a BP might have. It was shared by a reader with BPD named Julie:

Husband: Honey, I have a meeting so I can't take the kids to basketball practice.

Me: Can you reschedule, I always take them and it's your day.

My brain: He always breaks promises. It's like what I do is less important than what he does. Just because I don't bring in the money does not mean I don't work, etc., the anger starts to build. We start to argue and become even more angry.

Husband: I'm not going to do this all day. I'll reschedule.

You would think me and my brain would be at ease and happy that he agreed, but nope.

My brain: He is going to leave me. He is going to start flirting with his secretary who is cute and calm and thinks he hung the moon. Why did you flip out? Fix it NOW so he doesn't leave you.

Me: It's fine, don't cancel your meeting, I'll take the kids. Are tacos ok for dinner? I know they are your favorite.

For my marriage to Lyssa, the tacos were chocolate chip cookies that she whipped up from scratch to convince both of us things were okay. What are your tacos?

I mostly hear from men who have female BPs, so it stands out when I hear from a woman with a male BP. Rachel has done her homework and shared what she learned. She makes an excellent suggestion about how to prepare for a first session with a therapist:

My husband has narcissistic personality and borderline and psychopathy. I have spent about 10 to 12 years studying narcissism. I read about Borderlines when he was first diagnosed by a team of great psychiatrists and psychologists. I was fortunate to get him help, although there are no cures, there are medicines which help the raging which is one of the bad things. My husband has more traits of the narcissist and psychopath though, but there are some small things there too in the Borderline. One thing I will say here. If you are going to a psychologist or psychiatrist please take a list of the symptoms with you. I wrote out a whole book for the psychiatrist to go by when diagnosing my husband. I had been married to him at that time for about 16 or so years. The doctor thanked me afterword and said it makes their jobs easier in the long run as these people or patients will not volunteer any information or not much. My husband sat mute.

On a related note, my wife Lyssa and I had three different professionals suggest she had BPD, and as soon as they did, she cut off contact. The final therapist we saw was clever enough to avoid the term "BPD" and instead focused on "shame issues." That was the closest Lyssa got to admitting the bigger problem and trying to work on herself, but it didn't last too long.

Phil is a reader who wanted me to know that he found a path to a better life, but not without challenges:

I also experienced this "roller coaster" and I had no idea what it was until it was too late. I was sucked into the madness and tried to fix the Crazy which almost sucked me in to its black hole.

I have joint custody of my kids and I'm in an exceedingly happy place in life! There are no words to describe the inner-peace and joy that I feel right now.

Like Phil, I often hear from readers describing their kids as the biggest success of a BP marriage. Alexander agrees:

In hindsight, I don't even recognize who I was during the toxic marriage, and I see those days as some very dark times. The shining light for me is the birth of my kids. I don't even know why I stayed with her during the first year of marriage, yet now I see how the patterns of behavior confused/controlled me. Unfortunately, I didn't know about the existence of BPD prior to my kid's mother. I just thought it was due to immaturity or hormonal issues. I think I'm an expert on BPD now.

Alexander raises an interesting question. Most BP spouses get married *before* ever hearing about BPD. How many of us would enter into a relationship with a BP *after* we have learned all about it through real-life experience?

If you think about it, we'd be fairly effective partners to a new BP because we'd already be well along the learning curve. I think it is worth the effort to try and save an existing marriage, especially with kids involved. But to enter into a *new* relationship with a BP after having been in one previously? Would you do it?

Larry wrote me an extensive letter describing that falling for a BP can happen to even the most educated people:

My relationship has lasted 21 years, including marriage and 3 children. I'm divorced with my borderline ex and split with her 8 years ago. Although I am an attorney when we split, I spent the next 8 years pursuing a PhD in psychology where my focus was computational and behavioral neuroscience and even more particularly, BPD.

My ex was diagnosed with BPD and complex PTSD 7 years ago. Yet, we are still in court. We are in the middle of a custody battle. She has destroyed every relationship I have had since we split, forced me to lose two jobs, near bankruptcy, destroyed my personal and professional reputation. After 7 years of war in court, the judge finally realized she had been duped by my ex and awarded me sole legal/physical custody and ordered a custody evaluation by a psychologist. Since then, the judge has also issued a Domestic Violence Restraining Order against my ex to protect me and my children.

I'm sure the expense was worth it to Larry, but there are many BP spouses who simply don't have the resources to launch that level of a court battle, and their child custody results are far less satisfying.

He concluded his letter with the sentiments about having kids that I hear so often:

83

Looking back over the past 21 years with a very BPD educated mind, had I had that mind 21 years ago, I would have recognized her illness within about 9 months of starting to date. I would have run. I am glad I did not, else my children would not exist. I tell those close to me, "I slept with the devil to make 3 angels and the devil never sleeps."

CHAPTER 11: BUT WAIT, THERE'S MORE

Besides the basic symptoms discussed in the beginning of the book, there are a handful of other behaviors considered to be traits of borderline personality disorder. The BP in your life might not demonstrate all of them, but it pays to educate yourself on the possibilities.

There are no passages from readers in this chapter—it's just information I think you'd better have.

Risk Taking

BPs can be the ultimate members of the YOLO (you only live once) crowd. With an unstable or practically non-existent sense of self, a BP might pursue any number of dangerous activities in order to feel alive. These are actions purely for the thrill, rather than self-harm.

Prime examples include: one-night stands, group sex, extreme sports, starting fights in public, goading others to fight, gambling money they can't afford to lose, and aggressive driving.

Emptiness

The emptiness a BP feels is far more profound than what you and I experience. While we can hopefully convince ourselves that our feelings of emptiness are temporary, and therefore manageable, the BP considers them hopeless and infinite.

I could spot feelings of emptiness in Lyssa by her use of demonstratives. Like a toddler convinced the world is ending because of being told "no," a BP will shout, "I'll NEVER forgive you," and "You ALWAYS leave when I need you the most."

Mistrust

As you can imagine, if your spouse is constantly terrified of abandonment, they may not be able trust you. Trying to tell a BP that you love them is like quenching their thirst with an eyedropper. The moment you give them a drop, they immediately crave more. When you balk at delivering an endless supply, they mistrust your motives and attack you.

The moment you scratch an item off your list of "Things My Spouse Gets Upset About," they've added three more. And given enough time, any problem you think was handled in the past will come roaring back bigger and meaner for being ignored.

Interpersonal Sensitivity

Many BPs have the ability to quickly assess personality keystones in others and make use of the information to get what they need. This is extremely helpful in the workplace and allows BPs to succeed and be well liked.

I noticed this about Lyssa early on. She picked up on my signals, whether I knew I was sending them or not, and "magically" became increasingly attractive to me. Because she lacked a strong sense of self, she looked to me for ideas and embraced them for her own.

Control Issues

Often feeling helpless and without self-identity, a BP might overcompensate by aggressively trying to control people and situations around them. Following in the symptom of "extremes," the BP will see their world as either right or wrong. Everything is either in its place (on time, on budget, picture perfect, etc.), or it is wrong. No gray area.

I remember many frustrating occasions when Lyssa would accuse me of trying to control her reactions at the very moment her reactions were trying to control me. It was a vicious cycle. We would soon act like children trading silly reproaches like, "No I'm not. *You* are!"

Situational Competence

This symptom is very common among high-functioning BPs. While their personal relationships are a cesspool of disaster, the BP may be exceedingly successful in other areas. This is likely the case at school, work, athletics, or a serious hobby.

In this regard, the BP is taking control issues and focusing them on being productive. If you want a project done on time and near perfect, put a Borderline on the job.

Lyssa was brilliant as an artist. She would dedicate 6–8 hours a day to perfecting her craft and think nothing of it. This was easily the most impressive positive characteristic I saw in her personality.

Impaired self-direction

Conversely, a BP may enter phases where their life shatters and nothing gets accomplished. They think, "How can I worry about finding a job when life is meaningless?" The feelings of despair take over and can't be overridden.

Eventually, the mood swings the other direction and a phase of positive-minded productivity begins again.

Like I mentioned earlier, I learned that Lyssa would become severely impaired about every four days. Her goals for life would simply break like fragile glass against the unstoppable force of her depression.

In her fear, she would find a fault in anything I did and attack. It was never about me, but it sure felt like it at the time.

No Object Constancy

As adults, we have developed the skills to handle the absence of someone we care about. We miss them dearly, but understand that someday the feeling will recede. Not so the BP.

To them, they still cling to their infant-like belief that an object is not constant. If they can't keep an important item in the room, it's never coming back. Imagine how terrifying life is for your spouse when you dash out the door during an angry moment.

When Lyssa and I would argue and I would leave or refuse to interact with her, I would often find her laying on the floor surrounded by letters and cards I had written her. If she couldn't have me, at least she could try to confirm my existence (and therefore hers) with personal items I had given her.

The image of seeing her that way still breaks my heart all these years later. I just didn't understand what she was experiencing.

Narcissistic Demands

I have read that about 25% of BPs also have narcissistic personality disorder. The narcissist is known for constantly drawing attention back to themselves, especially in public.

Like a child throwing a tantrum, a BP will act out in movie theaters, stores, amusement parks, and church. They will want others to see and verify that you aren't being a caring, supportive spouse.

Lyssa's chosen locations for narcissistic episodes were amusement parks and department stores. The large crowds and abundance of triggering events made for a volatile cocktail of emotions.

Boundaries

Try setting a personal boundary with a BP and you will rapidly learn how much they don't like such things. Sentences that include "but" are a common trigger. "I love you, but..." "I know you'd like me to stay, but..." "This may feel acceptable to you, but..." All of these statements set boundaries. They draw lines that society says will activate consequences if you cross them.

In the all-or-nothing, right-or-wrong world of the BP, boundaries are meant to be blasted asunder in a fiery rage.

You'll need to learn how to set firm boundaries if your spouse has BPD, and be prepared to keep mending your scorched and splintered road block a thousand times.

CHAPTER 12: NEXT?

Some of the marketing materials for this book include the statement, "Like a graduate course for anyone trying to love or (for some of you) leave your BP spouse." If that's accurate (and I think it is), congratulations! You graduated from the course!

You've probably seen yourself repeatedly in the anecdotes of others shared here and found yourself shaking your head at the similarities. It's amazing, isn't it? All this time you thought you were the only one trapped in a crazy world, and it turns out there's a whole tribe out there holding a chair open for you in the clubhouse. Welcome! Come on in and have a seat at the big table.

Maybe you're like some of the others you've read about who are in the early stages of a relationship or marriage. With enough commitment and willingness by you and your spouse, it might work out. It definitely happens.

Or perhaps you've arrived at the closing curtain of a relationship and know there's nothing left to save. Your task will be to pick up those pieces like so many others before you and find a way back to the pre-BPD person you used to be. Figure out how to return to the path you were meant to be on.

Lastly, some of you are already free of a BP relationship but still rocked by the experience. It's okay to take the slow road to recovery. The bad dreams eventually diminish. The dire memories visit you less while in the shower. You'll stop expecting the "Crazy" to show up in anyone else you ever date. And if you're patient finding the right partner, you'll learn what you suspected to be true all along: when given the chance, you make a *great* spouse!

Just to prove that I don't think I have all the answers, I'm going to give a final passage to one of my readers who has BPD and wants non–BPs to be more open minded:

I don't think all of us borderlines are horrible partners and a waste of time. I think that like all relationships in life there just needs to be compromises and communication. And borderlines require a little more work than other relationships. Some of us borderlines make life more meaningful and interesting.

She's absolutely right.

Be well my friends. Be happy and healthy. And know that through all the mood swings, accusations, fears of abandonment, and threats of self–abuse, you weren't alone then, aren't alone now, and won't be alone tomorrow.

♦ ♦ ♦

Important Books from Robert Page
To visit my Amazon author page, simply scan this QR code into your phone or device and you'll see all my useful BPD titles:

Here are a couple specific books you should check out:

<u>Could Your Spouse Have Borderline Personality Disorder?</u> *<u>Understanding the Roses and Rage</u>*
This is a short-read, down and dirty "street-guide" to the symptoms of BPD and how you can spot them in your own marriage. Most spouses of a BP have no idea what they are facing and that they are not alone in their struggle.

<u>BPD from the Husbands POV:</u> *<u>The Roses and Rage of My Wife's</u>* <u>Borderline Personality Disorder</u>
There is finally a full-length book written *by* a husband of a "Borderline" *for* the husbands of Borderlines in non-clinical, compassionate, real-life language. Much more than an overview of BPD, you'll learn all about the disorder through the cringe-inducing but never mean-spirited accounts of Page's marriage to a BP. His "What I Wish I Had Done" revelations are invaluable!

What's Your Story?
As you read this book, you might have found yourself constantly recounting how your own BPD story has similar themes. I'd like to hear about it! Join the Facebook support group, <u>Roses and Rage:</u> <u>Spouses of Borderline Personality Disorder</u>, to share your experiences. I would especially love to hear from spouses who have found ways to reduce the BPD problems in your relationship.

Pass It On!

If you enjoyed this book and found it useful, I'd be very grateful if you'd **post an honest review** at the Amazon website. The more reviews, the higher the chances that others who need the book will see it.

To leave a review, all you need to do is visit the book's Amazon page. Scroll down and you'll see a button/link that says "Write a customer review" – click on that and you're good to go. While you're at the page, please "follow" me as an author so you'll be notified about future books.

Thank you for the support ~ Robert

In the eBook, you may click/tap here to leave a review.

OTHER RESOURCES

I am only presenting resources in this section that I have personally reviewed and found useful.

Arabi, Shahida. 2016. *Becoming the Narcissist's Nightmare: How to Devalue and Discard the Narcissist While Supplying Yourself.* CreateSpace Independent Publishing.

Borderline personality disorder. 2019. Article available online from the Mayo Clinic.

Borderline Personality Disorder. Undated public-domain pamphlet available from the National Institute of Mental Health.

DSM-IV and DSM-5 Criteria for the Personality Disorders. American Psychiatric Association.

Eddy, Bill. 2011. *Splitting: Protecting Yourself While Divorcing Someone with Borderline or Narcissistic Personality Disorder.* New Harbinger Publications.

Fjelstad, Margalis. 2014. *Stop Caretaking the Borderline or Narcissist: How to End the Drama and Get On with Life.* Rl Publishing.

Kreisman, Jerold, MD and Hal Straus. 2010. *I Hate You—Don't Leave Me: Understanding the Borderline Personality*. New York: Penguin Group.

Johnson, Merri Lisa. 2010. *Girl in Need of a Tourniquet: Memoir of a Borderline Personality*. Berkeley, CA: Seal Press.

Linehan, Marsha M. 2014. *DBT Training Skills Manuel*, 2nd ed. The Guilford Press.

Mason, Paul, MS and Randi Kreger. 2010. *Stop Walking on Eggshells: Taking Your Life Back When Someone You Care About Has Borderline Personality Disorder*, 2nd ed. Oakland, CA: New Harbinger Publications, Inc.

Stout, Martha. 2006. *The Sociopath Next Door*. Harmony Publishing.

ABOUT THE AUTHOR

Robert Page is my pen name when I write about BPD. I hold a doctorate degree in the Humanities from a fully accredited state university and have published several #1 Amazon best-sellers in non-fiction. After a decade in academia, I returned to my home-state roots to work in a dream job with the support of my second wife, family, and various rescue dogs.

Under my real name, I have written brief accounts of my experience with BPD, but the details in my Robert Page books are so revealing that it would be inappropriate for me to risk the anonymity of others against their wishes. Therefore, all the names (including the pets) and locations have been changed. Please follow my Robert Page Amazon Author page for more information.